Broken Heart Mosaics

Mosaicos de un Corazon Roto

A Bilingual Collection

A.L. Garcia

Broken Heart Mosaics / Mosaicos de un Corazon Roto
©2021, A.L. Garcia

27 Maryland St.
East Longmeadow, MA, 01028
413-433-0932
ALMAGARCIAL@yahoo.com

ISBN: 978-1-09836-247-8
ISBN eBook: 978-1-09836-248-5

Dedication

I dedicate this collection, first and foremost, to all those I have loved and/or lost on the journey I began thirteen years ago to heal my broken heart from the abuse I endured as a child. At twenty-one, I left my home and everyone I loved, in search of way to hold on to a hope I was very close to losing. For all the strangers who showed me kindness, friendship, or love along the way, I thank you. I dedicate this as well, as with all my writing, to my loving husband and two beautiful children. You three are a constant source of inspiration, support, and strength.

Dedicación

Dedico esta colección, ante todo, a todos aquellos a quienes he amado y/o perdido en el viaje que comencé hace trece años para sanar mi corazón roto del abuso que sufrí cuando era niño. A los veintiún años, salí de mi querida ciudad dejando atrás todos los que amaba, en busca de una esperanza que estaba muy cerca de perder. Por todos los extraños que me mostraron bondad, amistad o amor en el camino, se los agradezco con el alma. Dedico esto también, como con toda mi escritura, a mi amoroso esposo y a mis dos hermosos hijos. Ustedes tres son una fuente constante de inspiración, apoyo y fuerza.

Table of Contents // Tabla de Contenidos

ENGLISH SIDE // POEMAS EN INGLES

SPANISH SIDE // POEMAS EN ESPAÑOL

EXTRAS

Acknowledgements

I would like to acknowledge a few people by name who were of paramount importance to the editing process of this collection. I would like to thank Eva Alton, author of the *Vampires of Emberbury* Series, for her comments and suggestions. Your mastery of the Spanish language was especially appreciated. I want to acknowledge and thank Liv Houck for designing the weeping eye heart image in my front cover. I also send a special thanks out to my fellow creatives and poets, Tromonte Relford and Martingly Nelson. I am truly grateful to have met you both and know your thoughts on the flow, rhythm, and style of the poems. You are an inspirational pair of souls. I would also like to extend the most heartfelt thank you to a friend, former teacher, and fellow author, Michael F Deconzo. Having your support as a person and peer has been a blessing that I did not expect. Sixteen years ago, you gave a severely damaged child some hope, simply by talking about books with her. I will never forget that kindness. For as small as it may seem to many, it was lifesaving.

Finally, I want to express all my love and gratitude for the online writing community of Twitter and Instagram. Many of you have a strong grip on my heart and soul, for welcoming me into a world I did not know I would love. To the poets among you, #audrey2 vibes forever. All my best always, Alma.

Agradecimientos

Me gustaría reconocer a algunas personas que fueron de suma importancia para el proceso de edición de esta colección. Me gustaría dar las gracias a la autora Eva Alton, por sus comentarios y sugerencias. Su dominio de la lengua española fue especialmente apreciado. Quiero reconocer y agradecer a Liv Houck por diseñar la imagen del corazón con el ojo llorando en mi portada. También envío un agradecimiento especial a mis compañeros poetas Tromonte Relford y Martingly Nelson. Estoy verdaderamente agradecida de haberos conocido a ambos y conocer sus pensamientos sobre el flujo, el ritmo y el estilo de mis poemas. Son un par de almas inspiradoras. También me gustaría dar las gracias más sinceras a un amigo, antiguo maestro y compañero autor Michael F Deconzo. Tener su apoyo como persona y compañero ha sido una bendición que no esperaba. Hace dieciséis años, le diste una esperanza a un niño gravemente herida, simplemente hablando de libros con ella. Nunca olvidaré esa bondad. Por pequeño que parezca a muchos, me salvo la vida en muchas ocasiones.

Por último, quiero expresar todo mi amor y gratitud por la comunidad de escritura en las redes sociales de Twitter e Instagram por darme la bienvenida a un mundo que no sabía que me encantaría. Para los poetas entre vosotros, les envío vibras de #audrey2 siempre. Muchos de ustedes tienen un gran parte de mi corazón y mi alma. Todo mi amor y consideración, Alma.

Introduction

My love of literature, in all forms, began in early childhood as a way of escaping the abuse in my home. I am a survivor of child abuse, rape, and severe poverty. This is detailed in my personal narrative, published last year, *Broken Things*. I began writing poetry as a teenager to alleviate my rage and allow myself to dream. It has been my saving grace through myriad stages in my life, from serving in the military to finishing my education and becoming a mother. *Broken Heart Mosaics* is a hyper personal collection of poems reflecting this journey. I hope I may evoke in all of you who choose to read this collection, the same rollercoaster of emotions that overpowered me as I wrote them.

The extras are poems I posted on Twitter and Instagram as a part of the online writing community. They are similar in nature and are included here for the benefit of those who may not have an interest in or access to social media accounts.

Introducción

Mi amor por la literatura comenzó en la primera infancia como una forma de escapar del abuso en mi hogar. Soy una sobreviviente de abuso infantil, violación y pobreza severa. Esto se detalla en mi narrativa personal, publicada el año pasado, *Broken Things*. Empecé a escribir poesía cuando era adolescente para aliviar mi ira y permitirme soñar. Ha sido mi gracia salvadora a través de innumerables etapas en mi vida, desde servir en el ejército hasta terminar mi educación y convertirme en madre. *Mosaicos de un Corazón Roto* es una colección muy personal de poemas que reflejan este viaje. Espero poder evocar en todos los que eligen leer esta colección, la misma montaña rusa de emociones que me dominó al escribirlas.

Los extras son poemas que publico en Twitter e Instagram como parte de la comunidad de escritura en las redes sociales. Son de naturaleza similar y se incluyen aquí para el beneficio de aquellos que no tienen interés en o acceso a las cuentas de redes sociales.

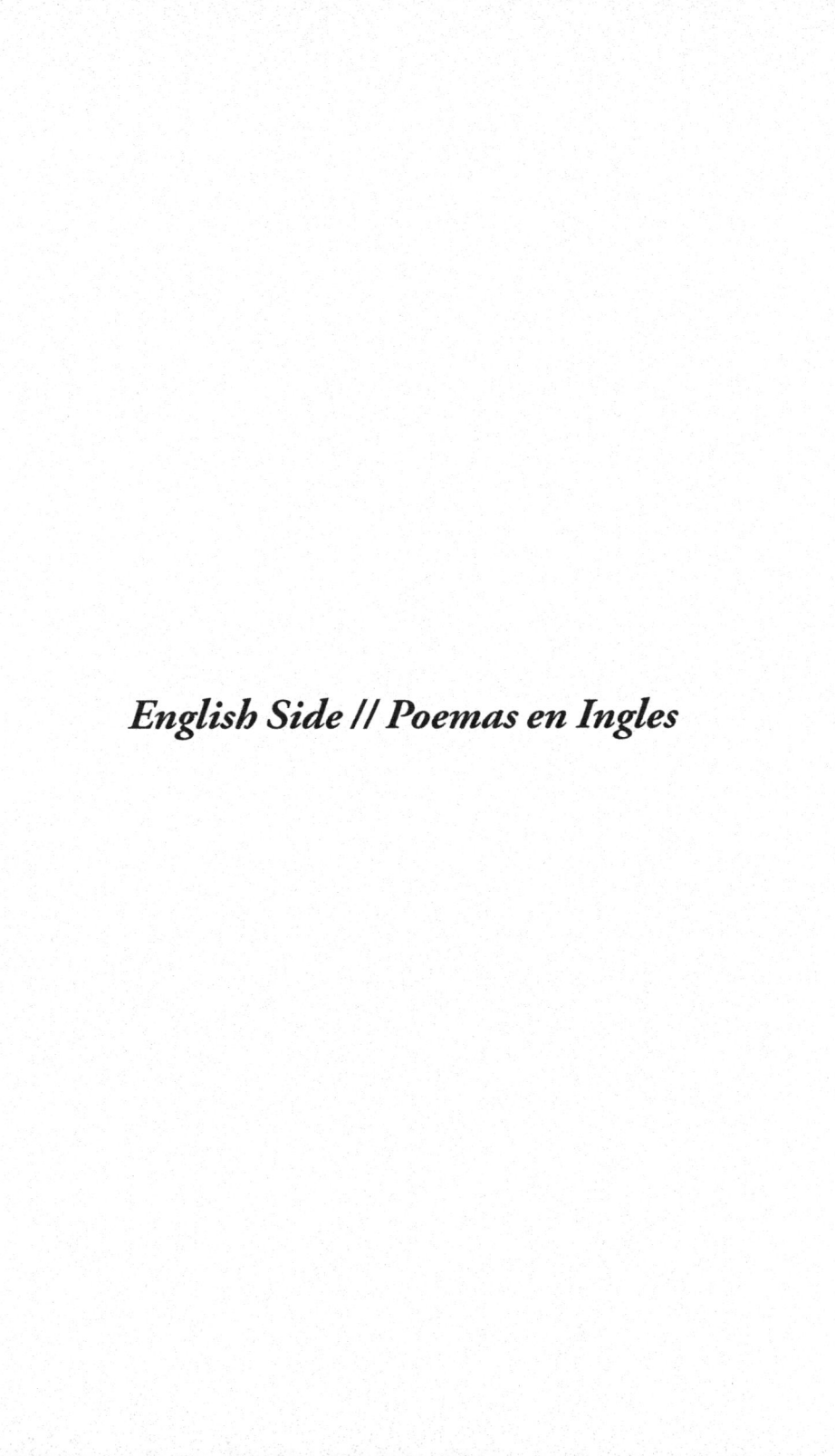

English Side // Poemas en Ingles

ZERO TO SIXTY, SIXTY TO NONE

Zero to Sixty, that's how my mind runs.
High on Life.
I'm the type of girl who soaks up the sun.
I live in that bright color, yellow,
And I am the mother who births out its mellow
Scenes, yearning to redeem
A heart that screams for justice, a mind that dares to dream.
Then. . .
I come crashing down like a stone, dropped from a skyscraper:
Pulverized bones.
PTSD,
That's what they call it.
Give me some meds to breathe while I'm falling.
I will never be normal,
That much I know,
But that's not what I need to feel whole.
They don't know what I need, though they like to pretend that they do
Experimenting with my life.
They want to Alpha-Stim me, so I can march in tune,
Another cog in the machine in need of a software reboot.
I think, even if they wiped my memory,
I would disappoint them,
Because I am a soul doomed to revelry and rage, with just a sprinkle
of sage.
A heart built to be as naïve as they come,
I love with the same fervor that my mind runs.
Zero to Sixty, Sixty to None.

FORGOTTEN STITCHES

I am certain I will die with my heart aching, bursting through seams I
have not secured well enough, in my never-ending efforts to stand and
be tough.

Perhaps snapped at an edge boasting the crude needlework of my youth,
the patches that I failed to mend. I know they shall be my end.
Running stitch holding in those wounds, lacking the embroidery I have
grown accustomed to.

They require skeins misplaced, lost with love that I have buried, deep
beneath the peace I married, many years ago.

These sutures were not whole when I abandoned them, and despite my
revamped skills, I have left them to fester,
Reluctant to repeat this knitting, a much more complicated quilting than
I care to work on.

My hands get tired now, my fingers tense, less nimble than they were
before, and more inclined to rest.

So, I sit and wait until they surface, wrapping them in dressings too thin
to hold back these tears.

DECEMBER

I was born into the heat of a dry season,
A couple of days before the longest day of the year,
Into sunny skies and sweltering air.

A warm December that my mind does not remember,
But she still calls my body to her grace.
A sweetness I dare not replace
With the winter storms I have endured.
I've been a winter baby here for so long.

Her muted skies seared in my memory,
Bleeding images of life, and love, and revelry,
Interwoven with those of my despair.
All my heartache, all my ravaged scenes,
She has been perennial in all these things.

Lulling me within her frozen breast,
Her frigid arms have long caressed my bones
When warmer nights betrayed this home.

Casting out a sun that beckons me
Toward the Southern Hemisphere,
Pleading me to bask in daylight,
Darken skin whose copper tones grow seasonally sallow.
They both call to me in their own way.

I follow.

A duality that molds my soul,
This daughter of the sun is anchored to the cold.

I AM THE BEGINNING OF THE END

I am   the
beginning of the end, leading   your fall into the depths.
I am the bleeding gut gurgling heartache of uncertainty, a solemn
persuasive song, stinking with the beauty of decay. I am the animation of
damnation, of blindfolded souls softly sagging away into the starry nights of
September. I am the screaming whispers of a paradise lost. I am the water of the
poisoned well when your mouth is parched with drought. I am that desperation,
and she is me, the lingering doubt in your throat. I am the frost on your last
remaining vine and the hopelessness that invades that precious mind. I am
your love rotting through a thousand lies and a million made up
memories dying to survive. I am the death of the song
of love. I am the sound it whimpers as it fades
and the silence that blooms in
its stay.

ALLOW ME TO MOURN YOU

Allow me to mourn you, love, let my heart close its wounds,
Seal up the memories, walk past the doom.
Allow me to bury your body, to give you one final kiss,
Cast off all those prior and leave you there with this.

Allow me to cremate these remains,
To turn this loss to ashes and let the wind carry them away.
Allow me to die to you today.
Let me extinguish the years, sink past those depths.
Allow me to mourn you, dear, and turn away from death.

FOR A BOY I LOVED

You are not the boy I loved, that tender-hearted prince that I survived
for, the one whose heart I chose over the sweeter proposal of death. At
the time, we were both children, when we swore to be as one; when we
spoke of the future, we had no idea who we'd become.

I am not that girl you loved. She is a cadaver too but not as
unremembered, I assume, as the corpse buried in you. A woman's in
her place instead, as steady as the one that's dead, and temperate as the
morning dew, unlike the child you once knew.

Perhaps you did not love me as I did you, or maybe I am just a fool,
In love with stories I once drew,
Meaningless but to our youth.

So now that I have told my tale, I'll leave you with one truth.
I still love that boy I loved, even if he isn't you.

IN MEMORIAM

Now the barren trees
Are bearing their winter wombs
Babes of December

Empty nests boasting
Children of the frozen breeze
They are blue like me

Bound to the barren
Bare flesh that once carried them
In memoriam

Soon they'll bleed again
The sweet sap of life blooms
Covering those tombs

Incinerated
But not so soon forgotten
In the summer breeze

The price of these
A sacrifice paid in full
At too high a cost

MEMORY OF MY LOVE

You are the memory of my love,
Unafraid, Unrelenting, and Inspired.
Full of amorous avarice and beating
A percussion of 99 beats per minute.
Breathing through my sweat, seeping
Through my breasts, a booming march,
Uncouth, Unsettling, and Loud.
Vivaciously Virile and Voluptuous.
The Renaissance painted in flesh,
Impaled on the branches of youth,
And lost to everything but its splendor.
Encased in desires with fantasies leaking from every gaze.
Pungent, Poignant, and Pervasive.
Forged by a miracle of mud and fire,
A man, unabashed and full of life.
Followed, accosted perhaps
By the fragrant dew of insatiable sensuality
Bathed in syllables of adoration.
Twitching still from its last encounter.
Proud and Painful, surrendered
Even against my will, to its might.

You love, are the memory of my love.
Of the sweetest lies,
Forever and forever and forever mine.

LOVE AND SLEEP

I miss lying down in love. I long for the naked sleepiness of my passion wrapped in the arms of another's fondness. I covet the grogginess of my soul sheathed in the lightheaded slumber of my heart at peace with the strength and warmth of skin and sweat.

I miss your love inside my love.

I yearn for the joyous grind of dreams that haunt me with the steady calm of an amorous omnipotence. My body clamors for the languid furnace of your hands as they roll politely through the nightmares in my breasts. I miss falling into your love, like the blossoms of cherry trees as they plunge into the breeze. Our promises captured in their petals, still only a fragile potential.

I miss these flashes of life in the mortuary that is existence without your touch. I miss your love and the sleep that lasted within it. For this inseparable slumber I wait. To sleep with you once more, once and forever more.

I AM A ZOMBIE

I am a zombie, addicted to brains.
Lost in thoughts and swimming in vain.
But I am not interested in escaping these waters.

Be my siren, serenade me with songs.
Sing me your lyrics, confess me your wrongs,
And sink me into the depths of enlightenment.
I will not rest until dark turns to light again.

Administer the antidote to ignorance.
Let not my mind exist in bliss.
Consign my eyes to observation,
And when I go blind from this,
Do not permit my release.

I am insatiable; feed me your logic.
Banish me to erudition,
Let your wisdom be my perdition.

Burst open your skull and seduce me.
I am ensnared by the truth it leaks.

Allow me to feed upon it,
Climaxing as I revisit your deeds
Feeding your own with my need for your refrains
Until nothing else remains

APRIL SHOWERS

For all those kisses you left on my lips,
Those April showers and all their sins,
These tokens of justice I must admit:
Your touch was as smooth as butter on toast.
When your love was a furnace,
I was its host,
As your skin echoed its velvety notes.
With your fingers perusing the depths of these bones,
I could stand unrobed against the cold staring down my demons,
And still feel whole
Because I was not alone.
I pushed you away because I despised myself
And you were too beautiful
To stand by that well of self-pity
That I had built in a world that was killing me.
Too perfect
To exist in a heart filled with black holes,
That I knew
Could suck up the rest of the souls in their vicinity
And leave me with nothing to offer,
And I could not live with that offer.

So, my dear lost lover, my April shower,
I wrote you this note to let you know,
That though our spring was so long ago,
I'll always hold on to those beautiful ghosts.

I DIDN'T ASK TO BE PRETTY TO YOU

I never asked for your attention.
I didn't know your intentions.
If that's what I had to go through,
I didn't ask to be pretty to you.

I never asked you for anything.
You didn't have to take all my things,
And break them and stain them,
And change who I was, who I'd be.

I'm not free,
From your shadows.
I'm not free from your shame.
Who's to blame for all this pain?

I didn't ask to be pretty to you.
I didn't need your affection.
I didn't ask for your attention.
If that's what I had to go through,
I didn't ask to be pretty to you.

You didn't ask for my permission,
Even though I couldn't give it,
When you did this.

For these things, you are not forgiven.
Did you assume I'd be forgiving?
Did you assume I was so giving?
When you did this,
When you created these wounds,
I didn't ask to be pretty to you.

If that's what I had to go through,
I didn't ask to be pretty to you.

And I am still fighting to be free,
From your shadows.
I still need to break free
From your shame.

I need to be free again
So I can be me again.

CARRIED

"Shut up and go to bed," my father yells, voice booming past the walls that divide us. Everyone closes their eyes as I lie here taking in the sounds, hearing muffled giggles turn to slow, deep breaths. The wind whistles by, spying on us carrying voices of others unknown to me. The wind carries broken things. They call for me to join them. Then comes the mechanical whir of the television turning off, as his footsteps slide toward the door, sandals hissing as they lift to take each step, and squeaking as they come back down. The doorknob clicks as it is turned, soft and steady like it's a secret. The door creaks as he slides in. He taps my shoulder and whispers, "Are you awake?" I don't respond, keeping my eyes closed, like I always do. He lifts me from the top bunk as I fall into his arms silently. Carried, like a broken thing. Carried, to be broken again.

THE PEN IS MIGHTIER THAN THE SWORD

The pen is mightier than the sword, revenge of all the ages born.
Scorned women do not write in vain. This is how I release my pain.
So, all the world might ever see, this truth I know shall set me free.
A snitch, a tattletale they'll say, but I won't let them stitch my brain.
No, not I, not evermore, taps the Raven at my door.
The pen is mightier than the sword.

This I believe and heals my soul and quells the anger in these bones.
A vengeance lost-past overdue, a courage I betrayed too soon.
Halted time and time again by shame, and pity and so much
fucking blame,
But shame will not halt this rebirth.
For as long as I have left on earth,
I'll find some time to speak a little more.
And prove:
The pen is mightier than the sword.

LOVE AND WORTH

Your love is the mirror
that salvaged my self-worth,
The stream that cleared the wreckage,
of my ill-fated birth.
Its worth cannot be measured
in miles or cents or words.
Nor is there an adage
that sums up all this truth.
Your selflessness released me
from decades of misuse.
This all-transforming power
that was your lover's curse.
Your curse and my salvation.
Your love and all I'm worth.

VOWS

Pebble by pebble
Drip by drop
The stone will be whittled
The ocean filled up
Penny by penny
From tip to top
The coffers turn plenty
The bread's built up
From corner to corner
With mitts and mops
The muck will be gathered
Away to the dumps
For where there is but love and trust
All the burdens turn to dust
So here is my oath, my word and my vow
I will stand with you, forever from now

HOMAGE TO THE PIE KING

The night before you got deployed, I flew across the country to see you,
when you were still that little boy, I still see in you.
We went to a Walmart for a couple of pots and pans,
And a little bit of food for an almost empty room.
Then,
we cooked, and we ate,
    and we talked,
        as if
            everything was
        not
              falling
                apart.
I remember laughing like hell,
Comfortable in the natural telepathy we had grown accustomed to,
Over years of being one another's right hand,
Over decades of ruling over our childhood wasteland,
As we listened to Clinkscales ramble on,
Somehow,
I knew this would soon be lost and you'd be gone.

So, I held your head in my lap, like I used to when we were young,
Thinking of that song we love,
and I stroked your hair while reading to you, clinging on to the boy I
once knew.

My Little Prince, my Pie King, my Twin Tower.
Your lonely scribe has relinquished her power,
But that night, she put up a fight,
For just a few more hours.

Our last hug came and went, and you went on your way.
You came back, and went back, and came back again,
but nothing was ever the same,
And
I have always taken the blame,
Because if only the universe had let you stay,
I would have died with a smile on my face,
If I could have taken your place,
So that you would not have had to change so much,
So that you'd still be that boy I love.

Your royal scribe, JstAGrl

FOR A

I gave birth to a Rose,
A rose from the Garden of Eden.
My Rose,
But not just a rose,
She is so much more than she knows.
A deity of moons, she is risen,
Shaped with the love that forged her existence.
She is a creature both miniature and grand,
Endowed with the light of her creators.
A daughter of these celestial truths,
She was born to bloom
Even within the darkness of the tombs
Her name was chosen to represent.
Her smile is the kind that can soften even death
With a countenance more precious than the porcelain faces
Of all the dolls I adored before her creation.
She is, and shall forever be,
Her mother's perpetual infatuation.

FOR E

I named you after power and gold, without really knowing that I was
doing so,
My Gilded King, My Hero, My Creator.
Through your birth, was spawned the worth of your maker.
Before you existed, I was just existing,
Only semi-alive,
But clinging to the love I had agreed to giving.
Then, you came bounding out from my womb,
Not yet one day old,
But commanding the room with a general's spirit and might,
You are the type that picks wars to fight.
I would soon learn what strong-willed could mean.
As stubborn as your mother has been, life sent me a captain to exile
my sins.
Your demands left me no time for sorrow,
But amid this compulsory healing of bones,
You were the engine that built up tomorrow.

Spanish Side // Poemas en español

MAMI LULA

Mi Madre Luz, mi Mami Lula.
Luz de mi vida, Mi Madre Luna.
Tu corazón como un sol, le da vida a la luna.
En tu jardín crecía el amor, porque en esa jungla, se despejaba la
amargura.

Mi Madre Luz, mi Luz de Luna.
Los resplandores de la mañana nacieron en tu cuna.
Con ese acento borinqueño, le sacabas risas a los días de lluvia,
y después con un salmo, arrullabas a las brujas.

Mi Mami Luz, Mi santa Lula.
Si existe luz en mi alma, es por reflejar la tuya.
Hace más de cinco años ya, tu regresaste al cielo,
y yo quede parada aquí en la esquina de mi duelo.
No entendía aun, que ya era tu tiempo,
que otros te esperaban en el reino de los sueños.

Siempre digo que soy hija de la Luna porque cuándo me encontraste,
a esta huérfana la hiciste hija tuya.

Mi Madre Luz, Mi Santa Lula.
Luz de mi vida, mi Madre Luna
Si existe Luz en mi Alma, es por reflejar la tuya.
Te amo Lula.

EL SOL Y EL CIELO

Un abuelo es un sol,
Una abuela, un cielo.
Son regalos de Dios,
Dos amigos sinceros.

De cerca o de lejos,
Nuestros seres queridos
Nos envían su amor
Mas allá del mar y los ríos.

Y los días pasan como agua
Entre nuestros dedos,
Y las fotos nos aguantan
Hasta que los vemos.

Un abuelo es un sol,
Una abuela, el cielo.
Dos almas prestadas
Del reino del universo.

EN LAS NUBES

Quiero vivir en una nube, la más alta y mojada del cielo,
Y suspirar el sudor de tu amor, en nuestra nube cerca del sol.
Y ahí, crear aguaceros de encanto que caigan sobre el agua y la tierra
Como ninfas embriagadas de mi locura.
Quiero endulzar mi lujuria con partículas de tu sensatez,
Y así crear sensaciones de querernos y amarnos a la vez.
Quisiera convertirme en flor de amapola y vestida así florecer,
Para supurar solamente placeres y endrogarte de la cabeza a los pies.
Como quisiera vivir en las nubes, en las nubes, saboreando tu piel.
En las nubes, mi cielo, en las nubes, en las nubes, cubierta de miel.

PARADA

Parada en la esquina de mi soledad, solía entretenerme con tu recuerdo. Apegada a las lágrimas de nuestra triste verdad, busco, pero no consigo el sueño, porque por las mañanas, yo miro hacia el cielo y encuentro en el tu rostro sonriente. Al vespertino, velo las estrellas, y el viento, en tus suspiros se convierte. Esta lejanía me ha destrozado el alma, estos recuerdos me enloquecen. Ya mis oraciones me fallan, se tiran por la ventana y desvanecen. Espero que regreses el mismo, que las maldades no logren convencerte, que recuerdes que eres mi principito, y que sientas estos brazos que quisieran sostenerte. Ahora sólo queda esperarte. En mis sueños te hallaré. De día, me toca extrañarte, y con esto me callaré.

OLVIDAME

Olvídame, que estoy perdida. Bórrame, para siempre de tu vida.

No me busques, que ya no existo. No me esperes, que nadie me ha visto.

Arrancaré de mi corazón, tu voz, y de mis labios tus besos. Y si no logro hacerlo, mi alma morirá intentándolo. Y aunque será con mi último suspiro, le gritaré al viento que te he olvidado. Al amor y a usted, les digo adiós, y con esto, se acaban los dos.

MIS RUINAS

Los llanos lloran por la distancia
Las cumbres lamentan su altitud
Las olas del mar por su abundancia
La tierra por su vicisitud
El centro del mundo se quema
El cielo se da por vencido
Los vientos se rebelan y todos caen sobre un mundo perdido
Toda la belleza de la tierra se ha extinguido
La felicidad que existía en ella, la he abandonado
Porque toda la pureza de los cielos se ha enviciado
Y la esperanza que dormía en mi alma, a ella también la han violado
Por estas ruinas estaré, hasta que me llame el sueño.

¿POR QUE TE ESPERO?

Aquí te espero sobre las piedras blancas del amanecer, piedras que me consumen la carne y se atrapan en mi piel. Te velo cada tarde con miradas llenas del solaz cristalino de mi ser, ocultando los desechos de tu ser. Piensas que pasará el tiempo como el viento, y que la nostalgia se irá, pero para mí, jamás. Jamás dejaré que el tiempo me prive del purgatorio de sentimientos que he elegido por esperar que vuelvas a mí, que sientas lo que yo sentí. ¿Por qué te espero con la mente en las nubes y los pies atados a las cenizas del ayer?

Porque eres la luz encarnizada de mi vida, aunque esté pintado de carbón ese corazón, un corazón que has llenado de espinas creadas por el mismo orgullo que ahora tomas de excusa para castigarme sentado en el velo de la razón, esa voz de la razón que antes ignorabas bajo el fuego insaciable de un cuerpo enloquecido con solamente besarte yo.

¿Por qué te espero, amor pasajero? ¿Por qué te espero, en los agujeros del dolor? ¿Por qué te espero?, Con el alma en duelo, en dulces desesperos por oír tu voz. ¿Por qué te espero, querido caramelo áspero? Aún espero sobre rocas sin color. ¿Por qué te espero, amado de mis sueños? Aún espero sobre rocas sin color. ¿Por qué te espero, amado de mis sueños? Porque yo espero que regreses vos.

PENSANDO

Pensando en el sol, las estrellas, la luna, la arena, en el paso de la tierra y mis manos con sus guerras, llenas de lápices gastados por escribir de tu amor. Los pistachos en mi mesa les sonríen a mis manos enyesadas sobre el pasto de tu adiós. Y los santos, y los dioses, y los gusanos que me consumirán me esperan con sus encantos y desencantos, llamándome otra vez a la oscuridad. Y todo esto sigue así, en las calles, en los campos, entre paredes y sin ellas, por un sin número de minutos que me quedan por correr. ¿Vale algo? ¿Vale nada? Vale siempre, y se acaba. Todo se acaba con la noche. Todo se enjuaga con tu voz. Todo se prende con el día. Todo se muere con tu amor. Te quiero. Te amo. Te odio. Te extraño. Me olvido, me alegro. Me enamoro, me daño.

VALOR

Lo que uno valora, no está para nadie decir,
porque lo que uno adora es el culto de uno solo,
y si alguno no lo entiende, pues, que se vuelva loco,
pero en su propio hoyo, para no estorbar a los demás.
¿A quién le debe de importar lo que otro quiera amar?
Lo que más falta en esta vida es amor de puro afán.
Y eso lo tienen, solamente, los que saben no juzgar.

GIRASOL

Tú eres mi girasol,
Esa especie de flor,
Que siempre mira hacia el sol,
Siempre con la frente en alto,
Aunque hayas pasado por un huracán devastador.
Tienes ese verdadero don,
Que prevalece en la isla del encanto.
Por eso eres un encanto.
Por eso te llamo mi Santo.
Mi Palo Santo.
Como esa madera sagrada,
La de mis antepasados,
La que quebraba las hachas del conquistador,
Y después se vestía de flores más brillantes que el sol.
Tienes el mismo aroma de pino dulce,
Ese incienso natural,
Por eso eres un amor que cura todo mal.
Mi santo de la isla del sol y el mar
Sólo te pido
Que nunca me dejes de amar.

DESNUDA CONVERSANDO CON LA TIERRA

A mí me gusta estar desnuda entre los campos al amanecer.
Me gusta permanecer desnuda, ahí,
Sintiéndome dueña de mis propios pies.

Descansa un rato, trigueñita, me dice la tierra,
Que te falta mucho por correr.
Cuando llegue el tiempo de partir conmigo,
Yo te daré la señal,
Y las fuerzas para arrancar
Hacia esas guerras frías que reclaman tu bondad,
Porque lo tuyo es amar, y amar sin descansar.
Aunque esta vida te enseñará mucho que odiar,
Las gotas de tu corazón serán como lluvia del Mar Muerto,
Llenas de sal, y hechas para purificar.
Tu corres con piernas de hierro y cal,
Y tu destino es destruir este mal.

No le respondo, pero me dejo llevar,
Cierro los ojos y repito:
Lo mío es amar, amar sin descansar.

Extras

POETRY-HEAD

I'm a poetry head, poetry is my crack;
Give me my medicine, pick up my slack.
Help me to survive another day
As my heart plays with the fruit of your muse;
The ink from your pens is the drug I abuse.
Take pity on this mortal addict,
Let not your heart turn to stone,
Bequeath a few more rhymes to these withering bones.
Let me breathe in your legacies,
Hide in your tomes.
Do not ignore my requests;
I am but a fiend for these enamored texts
Churned out by the beautiful minds of this new century.
I imbibe this mix of revelry and heartache
To heal this splintered soul whose home
Is, and will forever be, poetry.

MOSAIC HEART

My heart is a mosaic, patched up in a mended frame,
Glued together, painted over, and put back on display.
I am all the broken things of these exhumed remains,
That face of innocence, bludgeoned yet reclaimed,
But I am not the same.
A canvas reconstructed, and tempered to the shame,
Fearless now, as I was once,
To say what I must say,
To name who must be named.

FOR THE POETS

To be a poet is to live in dreams,
Of love, of loss, of liberty,
And all the moments in between,
To breathe in life and bleed it out,
In verse and rhyme and limerick.
And thus we share our great afflictions
With all the ones that choose to listen,
So, through these lines, you'll see my stitches.
To my fellow scribes, I do proclaim,
In your wounds, I will partake,
Even when it makes my heart ache.
Know this truth, as you are reading this:
This poor soul is always listening.

Leave me to my poems.
They are my closest friends.
They would not abandon me
When the sadness rears its head.
Leave me to these devices,
Pooling words of life, and love, and death.
Let me bathe inside these syllables,
And spare me all the rest.

Love, she is my saving grace.
In her name, time has not passed in vain;
The years have come and passed
But, as these petals and their thorns,
Past births and deaths,
They have remained. . .
Perennial.

I am crumbling like a strawberry shortcake
Beneath your gaze.
Look my way a few more times,
And I'm yours, babe.

I am not temperate when I'm in love.
I am smoldering.
Flaming fingertips soldering
Your skin with their touch,
Fusing your soul to mine.
My thirst for you is as insatiable as time.

I do not wear my heart on my sleeve; it's more like on a platter,
With a serving spoon on the side,
Ripe, raw, and willing you to take a bite.
But this caution I bequeath.
Like water for chocolate, she is seasoned with insanity,
The kind that asks for too much sacrifice.
Reciprocity will not suffice.
She demands eternal rights.

Swear to me the sweetest lies
That you are forever and forever
And forever mine
Even when you cease to exist
Promise me you will haunt my skin
Be a specter
Whispering songs in death
Frisson caressing me
In the absence of your breath

May our souls seek one another through all the universes that are or may come to be.

May they find the same hearts that swore themselves to infinity.

My affection is insufferable,
Cloying, in fact,
Urging you to throw it up,
Regurgitate my love
Because it is too much.

GILDED COIN

I am two sides of a gilded coin,
A self-deprecating joy,
Very vain, but still self-conscious,
Filled with rage but also kindness.
I am a contradiction,
A bit of all the works of fiction
I have consumed and that consume me,
Bittersweet to the core;
If you love the lady,
Love the whore.

TWO SIDES OF ME

My heart and soul are not the same.
My soul is another entity, not necessarily me.
She angers much more easily.
She tolerates no wounds,
And when she has been burned, I've had to pay the dues,
In flesh and blood, self-harm, so she would not harm you.
She wants the world to burn,
Fight battles I know are doomed,
And I can't always quell her pleas
With sweet reminders that we are free,
That we are loved,
That we are lucky to be alive,
That we should see how much we've risen,
But still my debts are not forgiven.

You owe me, she says,
And I intend to get my pay,
In flesh and blood if it must be;
The day will come when you are me.

SPRINTS

I went for some sprints
Now there's an ache in my bones.
This is the place I like to call home,
A dull aching, flesh tearing to tone
The weakness I hold.
I am free when I run.
I can breathe when my blood
Is coursing through my veins,
Melting away the pain.

RUN

I have to run like the hounds of hell are chasing me
Because my emotions, they run away with me,
And maybe if I run another thousand miles,
I might be able to take in another smile
Without my heart bursting to pieces.
I hold in my love that's always bleeding,
From my soul down into my soles;
I run to lighten the load.
Physically and metaphysically,
Enveloping my bones with the strength they are owed,
A peace that never grows old.

LETTER TO MY SOUL

I know you are angry at me for not having the strength to send those who
hurt you to hell.
I'm sorry.
I am not the supernova I know you must have been before you
became me.
I'm sorry for not believing in me when you needed me to see,
That the force of an entire universe lay with me, yearning to breathe free.

I am not afraid of what we could be,
But you've got to trust me.
The day will come when you are me.

One day, these mortal remains shall finally shatter.
One day, they will no longer matter,
And we will be what we are meant to be,
Something I could never be,

The energy of the stars being burned,
Of the sun melting into the earth,
Suffocating this life we have not earned,
Because now it is her turn

To destroy and build anew,
To revel in the joy of lost creations,
A symphony of revelations,

As we shed our skin sheaths
With our humanity bursting at the seams,
Holding one another as we all become dreams,
As our hatred is incinerated and scattered in the breeze,

With all our love, and all our rage,
And everything in between
Finally, free just existing,
Without the cages of minds they have been living in.

Trust me,
I am not afraid of what we could be.
The day will come when you are me.

SHOULD HAVE, COULD HAVE, WOULD HAVE

You should have been my mother.
You could have been my closest friend.
I would have given anything for you to take my place.
To be the object of his obsessions,
As I could see he was to you.
I wish you would have seen this truth.

PURGATORY

She's too sensitive
She has too many triggers
Dealing with her is an impossible mission
She dreams in nightmares
Too many visions of a past still in that reel
Hauntings that still feel too real
Some nights
She is still that little girl left in the dark
With all of her worries and a little less spark
Seems she's been through too much
To end up so tough
So she survives for another generation
The ones that she holds in her arms
Holds on so that they can be all that she isn't
No tragedies lingering in their sides
No way to relate to that side of their creator
She will rejoice if they are not like their maker
She is a sinner
They are her saints
So she gets up and puts on the war paint
Determined to live just one more day
Every day.

Nah, fuck all that.
Weapon of choice: melee
I am still as buck wild as they come
And I'm ready to slay
Poetess by day and just a bit insane
By night I am devoured by flames
My soul is but the ashes that remain
Of a dame who is not afraid of her demons

Or the devil to boot
They are not eviler than what I've lived through
This is the purgatory game I play
In her name

HE FORGETS

He forgets how much I need him
How easily my heart folds beneath his
How vulnerable my skin is to his touch
He sees a sallow flat veneer
But I am not what I appear
With just one tap
I'd let him in
If he'd absolve me of my sins

MISERY

They say misery loves company,
As if she were a bitch,
As if she didn't need someone to sync with.

Tragedy befalls us all,
We all know that.

So, as misery comes and goes,
And we take our turns,
Let us not forget,
Our soul is reflected in the way we lie with her

LOOKING UP

Always looking up, I remain unbothered.
My heart is one that's been tested through fire.
I breathe with lungs burning with passion.
I dream of worlds where love runs rampant.
I run like the wings of a Pheonix are holding me,
Wrapped in an embrace of all that emboldens me,
My feet striking earth,
My head in the clouds.
I am the angel that rules this holy ground.

A face matches a voice, and we are human again.
A conversation fills the void that time had filled in
Around the humanity that our bodies hold
When we are close enough to feel our minds beating,
To hear our hearts speaking,
To see the human side to this world with no end.
A stranger is just a friend lost to the wind.
A friend is just a stranger you pulled back in.

SNOW

The snowfall holds memories we never took pictures of.
Icy fingers warming one another's up.
Frozen breaths lingering with love.
These dormant trees, our sole spectators,
Historians of the storms we've weathered,
Chronicling the unremembered dreams
We walked away from
As Logic took their place.
She has robbed us of this space,
Where we once shared our souls
Beneath the falling snow.

Rip my heart to shreds
Burn the strings connecting it to you
Just don't leave me in silence
This awful solemn end
You seem to assume is kindness

SILENCE

The quiet ones
Are the ones that kill you.
Unassuming bastards
That are always calm.

He does not cry like me.
He forgets I have hand sewn his seams.
So, he remains
Stoic-faced till death.

His muted heart,
With its lost soliloquies,
Is far harsher than it seems to be.

You told me once when we were young
You dreamt of me before we met.
It was as if you had conjured me
Up and out of the bottomless pit
I called home,
Willing me to live, demanding.
And for all my trying,
I could not abandon it.
I wonder now, as I grow old,
Where did my sweet sorcerer go?

I know I lost you on the road
But I assumed I'd paid my tolls.
So why am I still tortured?
Have I not waxed poetic long enough?
Have I not wept upon the grave of our love?
Have I not left us flowers?
Didn't I relinquish all my power
For your well-being?
Love, why won't you let me go?
When, I pray,
Will you release me from these woes?

YOU USED TO WRITE ME LETTERS

You used to write me love letters.
Long amusing notes,
Filled with nicknames for my soul.
Starburst Fire, Soldier Girl.

Thus, you penned the dreams of our resistance
Before the reckoning of my distance
Came to collect its dues,
The miles between us blackening our youth,

And altering your gaze,
As I made myself the martyr
To release you from your duty to my praise.
But you could not do the same.

This gift was not yours to give.
You were unaware.
You were my first.
My first lover, my first true friend.
The heart you have forgotten
Is what was willing mine to live.

I don't like anything half-assed.
So, if that is all you have to offer,
Leave my obsessive ass alone.
Go find another set of bones
Willing to accept your scraps.

If you can't love me harder,
Then don't even bother
To knock down these walls.

Did you know?
They house roses that will never wilt
Because they are watered
With my own flesh and blood,

And sowed upon a sacred ground.
Protectors of this owner's crown.
Now,
Would you still dare to tear them down?

And assume you have no price to pay
For disturbing my remains?

I ate so many of my feelings
I lost my appetite
For apathy

I do not want to be dead inside
Though it may be a blessing.
I've always chosen love over everything.

It is not an affliction I consider changing.

I dream
Of a world overrun by poetry
Troubadours on every corner
Conversations filled with rhythm and rhyme
Iambic Pentameter
The whole nine
Filling the streets with their cries
Like tidal waves of inspired minds
Crashing over space and time
Humanity seeping through our pores
As the syllables pour
And poetry reigns
Over all my days

For the Readers

If you enjoyed my poems, I would be truly grateful were you to take the time to leave a quick review on Amazon or Goodreads. As an indie author, I need reviews to help get my work noticed. Please feel free to follow my social media accounts or website listed below. I am always posting original poems there and would love to hear your thoughts.

Para Los Lectores

Si disfrutaron de mis poemas, agradecería mucho si tomaran un momento para dejar su crítica en Amazon. Como autora independiente, esto ayuda a que mi trabajo se destaque. Por favor, no dude en seguir mis cuentas de redes sociales o sitio web que se enumeran a continuación. Siempre estoy publicando poemas originales allí y me encantaría escuchar sus pensamientos.

Website: **https://www.brokenheartmosaic.com**
Twitter: **https://twitter.com/ALGarcix**
Instagram: **https://www.instagram.com/algarcix/**
Facebook: **https://www.facebook.com/almagarcix**